VANISHING CULTURES

FAR NORTH

JAN REYNOLDS

LEE & LOW BOOKS INC. • NEW YORK

To my grandparents

and all wise elders around the world—J.R.

LEE & LOW BOOKS Inc., 95 Madison Avenue, New York, NY 10016
leeandlow.com

Manufactured in China by Jade Productions, March 2013

Photographic work supported by the Professional Photography Division of Eastman Kodak Co.

Original design by Camilla Filancia
Lee & Low Edition design by Rich Deas
Book production by The Kids at Our House

The text is set in Palatino

1 2 3 4 5 6 7 8 9 10 (HC)   10 9 8 7 6 5 4 3 2 (PB)
First Lee & Low Books Inc. Edition, 2007

Library of Congress Cataloging-in-Publication Data
Reynolds, Jan.
Far north : vanishing cultures / by Jan Reynolds. — 1st Lee & Low Books ed.
p. cm.
Originally published: San Diego : Harcourt Brace Jovanovich, ©1992.
Summary: "Describes, in text and photographs, the vanishing culture of the Samis, the reindeer herders of the land
in the far north called Finmark"—Provided by publisher.
ISBN-13: 978-1-60060-142-2 (hardcover)   ISBN-13: 978-1-60060-127-9 (paperback)
1. Sami (European people)—Juvenile literature. I. Title.
DL42.L36R49 2007
948.97'7—dc22   2006029269

The Samis live in a land of the far north called Finmark, or Lapland, where the sun can sometimes shine all day and night during the summer and sometimes not shine at all in the winter. They make their shelters by wrapping heavy cloth around poles made from trees, which are then fastened together at the top. For thousands of years, the Samis have followed the migration of the reindeer across the plateaus and up into the mountains in the summer then back down to the plateaus in the winter. Following the natural cycle of the seasons, they believe that nature will always care for them.

But this ancient way of life is disappearing as new roads and towns change the landscape, and helicopters and snowmobiles replace the Samis' traditional methods of reindeer herding.

We and the Samis are all part of the same human family, and the loss of the Samis' traditional way of life is our loss, too. Like the Samis, we all depend on the natural world to live. We all share this earth, its lands and waters. And because of this, perhaps we should take a look at the Samis' life in harmony with nature before it vanishes forever.

There is a place in the far north where the sun can stay up in the sky all day and all night. It is called the land of the midnight sun.

In the chill of the evening, when the sun hangs low, Sara and Kari, two Sami girls, draw closer to the fire as their mother begins to tell them a story.

"Like all Samis, she lived her life close to the rhythm of the land and animals, following the circle of the changing seasons. In the warmth of summer, when the sun shone all day and night, life was good in the mountains. But in the dark cold of winter, when the sun sometimes did not rise at all, she and the reindeer would return to the lowlands where winter was more gentle.

"Long ago your grandmother followed the reindeer as they traveled up into the mountains for the green summer grass in the high pastures.

Reindeer-skin drum with antler drumstick

"The Sami shaman seems to be the first to know when the seasons will change. The shaman believes the trees, rocks, and waters all around have their own spirits. And with the help of his drum, he talks with these spirits to find answers for the Samis."

Soon Sara and Kari are fast asleep.

It is early spring, and Sara and Kari's father is out rounding up the family's reindeer. Like their grandmother, Sara and Kari will travel with the reindeer up into the high mountains.

The next day, while the girls wait for their father to return, Kari gathers small berries as a treat for the family. After gathering the fruit, she hangs reindeer skins out to dry.

Reindeer are the center of Sami life. Their hides are used for clothing and blankets, their meat for food, and they pull the sledges the Samis ride across the snow. The Samis also drink the nourishing liquid from inside the reindeer bones. Then they carve the bones to make spoons, needles, and other things they need.

When their father arrives, the girls help their mother take down the *lavvo*, their simple tent, and get ready for moving to the mountains.

Kari is happy to see her favorite dog again. He is very good at herding and always goes with Kari's father to gather the reindeer.

When the reindeer are rounded up, they must be fed. Sara and Kari set out some hay for their father to take to the herd. While the girls are busy, their father goes to get a sledge to carry the hay on.

Although the sun is still up, it is nighttime. After helping her mother and sister pack their belongings onto sledges, Kari falls asleep on an empty sledge.

The family will begin moving later in the night when the sun is even lower, and the air becomes colder. Then, as the snow freezes harder, the sledges will slide faster and more easily.

While Kari and her sister sleep, their father takes hay out for the reindeer to eat.

During the winter, when the reindeer are allowed to roam freely, they eat lichen, a small plant they dig up from under the snow with their hooves.

After the reindeer have eaten, Father brings in the strongest one to harness to the sledge. It is time to begin moving to the mountains. Kari and Sara like to ride with their father, listening to him *yoiking*, singing traditional Sami poetry.

Occasionally they stop to let the reindeer rest and graze where the spring sun has melted away the snow. As they follow the herd, their father reminds them of what Samis have always believed: Nature will care for them as it does all living things.

The traditional Samis look forward to living high in the mountains for the summer. Some will stay in a *goatti*, a hut, instead of the lavvo. After the snow melts, all the different families' reindeer herds will graze together in the high pastures. The animals will grow strong and healthy, which will help them through the long winter to come.

By the end of summer, the adult reindeer will have shed their old antlers. They will have soft, new ones covered with velvet, a fuzzy skin that falls off when the antlers become hard bone. Along with their new calves, they will be herded into a large corral. This is when the calves' ears are marked.

Each Sami family has its own mark, and the children in each family have their own marks, too. These earmarks are important. Each family will use them to separate its reindeer from all the rest when it's time to leave the mountains and travel back to the lowlands for the winter.

Sara and Kari can spot their family's animals from a distance. While Sara helps her father, she points to a lone reindeer and asks Kari to check the ear marking. Kari calls back, "This is your reindeer, Sara."

Before Sara and Kari reach the mountains and high pastures, there is still more traveling to do. Mother has already gone ahead with other Samis to prepare the lavvos at a resting place.

While the girls are helping their father with the reindeer, their mother gathers wood for the fire and makes a pot of stew. She knows her family will be hungry when they arrive.

Like Kari and Sara and their family, other Samis are also herding their reindeer to the mountain pastures. As the different families arrive, they begin to gather for the big spring celebration.

Every year the Samis celebrate the end of the long, cold, dark winter. They dress in beautiful woolen and deerskin clothes covered with decorative hand-woven braid.

Reindeer-skin shoes

Left page: Traveling under the midnight sun

Lasso-throwing contest

Everyone is happy. The spring celebration is a time for friends who haven't seen each other for a long time to talk and laugh together. There are games, too.

Over his shoulder, Father carries his favorite blue lasso, a special rope used to catch reindeer. He will compete against others in a contest to see who can throw their lasso the best.

Sara and Kari make their own game. They turn in circles to see how far they can spin their skirts out, laughing as they make themselves dizzy.

But the most exciting part of the celebration is the reindeer race. Both men and women compete together, and Sara and Kari's mother is going to race this year. She carefully checks her sledge to make sure everything is ready.

Far out across the snow, the Samis race their reindeer. It is hard to tell who is winning at first. But as the racers get closer, it looks like a young man might win. Then, suddenly, Mother's reindeer bursts into the lead and crosses the finish line.

Kari and Sara are happy their mother won the race. They are very proud of their strong reindeer — and to be Samis living in the far north.

Ever since I was a child, I have been fascinated by the Samis who live in the far north, above the Arctic Circle in the upper reaches of Scandinavia. These people have been living in peaceful harmony with nature for thousands of years. I am especially intrigued by Sami shamans, who are beautiful examples of the basic Sami belief that nature will always care for them—when a shaman beats his drum, he enters into conversation with all the spirits of nature to receive knowledge. I had always hoped to some-day meet these people. However, what first brought me to the land of the Samis, the land of the midnight sun, was neither the Samis nor their shamans, but a nuclear di-saster. I went to Finmark to report on how one of the world's ancient cultures, inseparable from the earth and her natural cycles, was being directly altered by the nu-clear age.

The year before my first trip, a wind from the southeast brought a deadly rain over the far north. The unsuspecting Samis had no idea that a nuclear power plant in Chernobyl, in what is now the Ukraine, had exploded, sending radio-active poisons thousands of meters into the atmosphere. This radioactive material soon rained down on the Samis, their animals, and their wilderness. The first news was that the radioactivity had poisoned everything—water, forests, all of nature, everything the Sami life was built upon. The Samis had lived through hard winters before when part of their reindeer herds had died. They understood and accepted natural disasters. But to these people, it was difficult to accept that their apparently healthy reindeer could be deadly because of radioactive contamination, and that the beautiful, life-sustaining land they lived on could be considered a death zone.

Unlike elk and moose, the reindeer's diet during the winter consists of raovvi, a lichen without roots. Because this lichen is slow to flush and cleanse its rootless system, the reindeer risked reingesting the water-soluble, cancer-causing radioactivity year after year. With their animals, food, land, and water contaminated, the Samis' tradi-tional ways appeared to be threatened. Although an in-credible number of contaminated reindeer had been destroyed and buried in mass graves, when the Swedish government tested the herds to determine safe levels of contamination, they discovered that the reindeer with lower radiation levels were, in fact, slowly cleansing them-selves. Some herds were even trucked to cleaner pastures to survive. Although it would take years, the herd would continue, and the Samis could rebuild their life with the reindeer.

During the return trips I made to this region following my study of the effects of Chernobyl, I was able to share in the rich culture of the Samis, a people who have lived in this area perhaps since the time the ice receded from the land. Although almost nothing of their heritage has been written down, the pattern of their lives is well known: throughout the years their way of life has re-mained the same because of their reliance on the reindeer. In the summer, the reindeer migrate higher into the mountains to graze, and in the fall, they return to the lower plateaus and are separated into groups for rutting. In the winter, the reindeer graze snow-covered pine heaths for raovvi by digging through the crust with their hooves. The physical boundaries of the Samis' land and the rhythm of their lives are set by natural forces and the instinctive migration of the reindeer, not by politics and economics.

For the traditional Samis, the reindeer have always been the ridgepole of life. These people ate no bread, only meat, milk, and cheese from their deer. Hides were used for clothing, and bones for utensils. Even the birch bark covered lavvos were sewn with reindeer sinews. Along with providing food, transportation, and clothing, the reindeer played a central role in cultural ceremonies. For example, when a suitor came in search of marriage, he circled his lover's lavvo with his reindeer and sledge, and if the woman stepped out and unharnessed the reindeer, he could proceed with the courting. When the two lovers exchanged draft deer, they were engaged.

I was fortunate enough to be lovingly taken in by the Utsi family, who are still holding onto some of the older Sami traditions. I first met Karen Utsi, Sara and Kari's mother, at the spring celebration. Although I spoke no Sami, and she spoke no English, we shared a common language, Norwegian. She jovially invited me to share a meal with her and her family in their lavvo. While cooking reindeer stew in a big, black pot hung over an open fire, Karen told me she was born in a lavvo just like the one we were sitting in. As we waited for the family to arrive on the sledges, Karen told me her fondest memory as a child: moving the reindeer during the long summer nights under the dim, low-lying sun. To her it was magical, almost like living in a dream to be so tired, yet so happy, up all night out in the wilds of the plateau. After spending time with Karen, I came to admire her strength and good humor despite adversity (although the cause couldn't be precisely determined, Karen's husband had recently lost his stomach to cancer). I could tell she was a strong woman, and I could see why some people believe that the Samis were a matriarchal society. And I can believe the stories that have been passed down through the years that a Sami woman might leave her child suspended in a reindeer skin in a tree with a marrow bone to suck on, so she could join or lead the hunts.

One day we were picking spring berries that grow in the open patches of vegetation that appear on the tundra, which look like green islands in a sea of snow. The sun was now up almost around the clock, and the weather was quite warm and pleasant. After eating our fill of berries, we climbed onto the sledges to travel home. Kari's father handed her the reins and jumped on behind me, then he began yoiking, singing Sami poems, with warmth and contentment. The sun was bright, the snow was fast, the sledge was swift, and we were happy. A feeling of serenity ran through me, and I was left with a deep respect and appreciation for the interconnection of the Samis' lives with all things in nature. I began to see that all people are inseparable from the land. And when the last traditional Samis are gone, it means more than the disappearance of a way of life: it's the loss of humankind in deep harmony with nature, at peace with their world.

—Jan Reynolds